Mental MakeOver
Creating a Positive Mindset
Quote Book

KELLEY R. PORTER
Award Winning Author, Speaker and Coach

KELLEY R PORTER, CERTIFIED LIFE COACH

ALSO BY KELLEY (Kelly) R. PORTER

Perfectly Planned (Overcoming Incest, Rape & Sexual Abuse)

Perfectly Planned Workbook and Audiobook

Overcoming Toxic Relationships (Creating Power from Past Pain)

It's All About Life (Book of Poems)

Detox or DIEt (Closing the Gap Between Dis-Ease & Death)

Copyrights © 2015
All rights reserved. Printed in the United States of America. No part of this book may be used or reproduced in any manner whatsoever without written permission except in the case of brief quotation embodied in critical articles and reviews.

Cover Design by Kelley R. Porter
ISBN: 978-0-9851767-5-4

PORTER PUBLISHING
TRANSFORMING LIVES WORLDWIDE

Dedication

Thinkers
Doers
Winners
Healers
Mothers
Fathers
Wives
Husbands
Authors
Speakers
Entrepreneurs
People of the World

Acknowledgments

A special praise and honor to the Universe and those who were a part of my teachings and studies. My life has become enriched with such magnitude and the greatest thing I can ever do is to give back what I have learned.

Special thanks and love to
Patrick O. Turner (Husband)
Dr. Anthony Gantt (Business Coach)
Rita Stewart (Professor)

Contents of Quotes

1. Self-Reflection 1
2. Life 20
3. Love 39
4. Inspirational 54
5. Relationship 65
6. Motivational 79
7. Business 97
8. Health 120
9. Abuse 134
10. Forgiveness 143
11. Featured Bonus 154
    (10 Ways to Release Negative Thoughts)

Self-Reflection Quotes

"Insecurities are unfortunate self-doubts either originating from growing up in a dysfunctional household or experiencing betrayal and deceit as an adult."

"You're jealous because you don't believe you can have what others have as you haven't recognized the greatness in you that you see in others."

"Living on defense is silently living in fear as you assume everyone is out to get you."

"When we assume someone is trying to hurt or attack us, we respond by attacking back. Imagine if that person was never there to hurt you."

"The more you criticize any individual, the more you should use every opportunity to self-reflect and identify the parts of you that need healing."

"Criticizing others says nothing of them and everything about you."

"Do some time in the mirror so you can see who you are and not what you look like."

"Comparing self to others is a definite way to demolish your confidence."

"If standing in your truth is difficult, it must take a lot of courage to live a lie."

"Money, make-up, fashion & bling can do many things, but it can never repair a wounded soul."

"It's okay to have all the 'things' you want in life, but don't spend money on things as a way to make you feel better; it's like putting a band-aid on a concussion."

"The company you keep determines the trouble you meet."

"If your character is built on your currency, more than likely you are emotionally and spiritually bankrupt."

"When you are comfortable in your skin, you do not require societal acceptance or approval."

"To love and accept self, you cannot hate the experiences that created you."

"Never downgrade or upgrade yourself to satisfy anyone, or any group of people."

"Stop being so exceptional at following the "in crowd" and become exceptional at being yourself."

"Connecting with your inner-self before connecting with others is a great way to display who you truly are."

Life Quotes

"If you aren't grateful for what you have, don't expect to receive more."

"Every tear shed is a sign of strength and freedom to come."

"Your past cannot be altered or erased; it can only be accepted and embraced."

"Your past experiences are purely lessons meant to teach self-knowledge & unconditional self-love."

"Life is never difficult or shitty as it is your stinkin thinkin."

"Only you can change your life; no one can do it for you."

"To conceal a painful past is to escalate stored anger and prevent liberation."

"Your buried pain is a concealed weapon to those closest to you."

"Sometimes our best days are the ones in which we just go with the flow and allow the day to take us by the hand and capture our spontaneous hearts."

"Your mind is the foundation of your life; when you fill it with positive thoughts, you will transform your life."

"Don't allow a temporary problem to be the reason you permanently give up on life."

"Life goes on whether you choose to live in the past or move forward."

Life doesn't require you not to fail, but to fail, get up and try again."

"Life is best spent in the present moment."

"The life you planned wasn't yours to begin with so let it go and create the one that is waiting for you."

"Once you realize that you are a creator and your experiences are directly related to your mentality, you will then shift your paradigm."

"You learn who you are and have been through the outcome of your children."

"Create a life you love, and you will spend every day on vacation."

Love Quotes

"Deeply loving and trusting others provides courage."

"Love is vulnerability."

Kelley Porter

"Love is never giving up on you."

"Love is an essential food for the mind, body and soul."

"Love is giving and not expecting anything in return."

"Love is when you trust the process of life and appreciate all your experiences."

"Love begins with not attempting to change those we love. In doing so, we only love the image of us that we see within them."

"The way you love yourself is the same you others will love you."

"Love is loving your flaws, mistakes, past, sarcasm, darkness and everything that scares you."

"People express love with the resources they have, not by how you think they should love."

Kelley Porter

"Love is giving in and taking the high road."

"Love is not being afraid to let go."

"The love you receive is the love you think you deserve."

"Accepting everything about you including your dark side is a part of loving self."

Kelley Porter

Inspirational Quotes

"Be open to the unknown as it shows great courage."

"Don't be afraid to show and wear your flaws as they are bigger than your mindset can see. Your shame and embarrassment hinders your inner and spiritual growth."

"You are a gift to the world and if your thoughts speak otherwise, channel them and affirm greatness."

"Everything is not a lesson. Sometimes people are showing you who they are and who you are; believe them."

"When you refuse to accept and embrace your experiences, you consciously choose to live in pain."

"Please remove the victim mentality or you will subconsciously push people away that may come close to your heart."

"When life knocks you on your knees don't get mad, create a better experience."

"Live in your truth regardless of what people think."

"Look forward to meeting the next breakthrough and defeating the next breakdown."

"Expect and welcome obstacles and challenges, don't avoid or resist them as these experiences make us better people."

Relationship Quotes

"Never allow the sins of another to make you doubt yourself, change your heart or avoid relationships."

"Love is not found between a man's legs, look within yourself."

"Ninety-seven percent of relationships are meetings of the Ego's."

"Follow a man with direction, not just an erection."

"If you find yourself experiencing the same relationship over and over again, you missed the lesson in the first relationship."

"You must be happy to attract happy."

"The people you are in relationships with are there to show you who you are if you choose to look internally instead of externally."

"Self-approval and self-acceptance are keys to great relationships."

"If you want a phenomenal and fascinating relationship, then you need to bring your phenomenal and fascinating self."

"The best thing to spend on any relationship is time, communication, compassion, honesty and understanding, not money."

"There is only one ingredient needed to destroy any relationship, and that is your Ego. The healing ingredient is to let it "go" by removing the e."

"There are many lonely people in marriages."

"Being in a relationship with you means to be in joy and satisfaction with self as it doesn't mean to be alone."

Mental MakeOver   Creating A Positive Mindset

Motivational Quotes

"Stop trying to cross bridges that need burning."

"Ask for help; it doesn't mean you fail, it means your refuse to fail."

"If you spent the same amount of energy on personal development as you do working for others, you would be spiritually wealthy."

"Don't attempt to be better than anyone else, be better than you thought you could ever be."

"Acknowledge your fears as you are the one who created them."

"Don't become a skeleton trying to help and fight for those who do not think their life is worthy."

"The energy behind fear should never be nurtured. Instead, nurture those emotions and behaviors that excite and elevate your life."

"If your behaviors, patterns, and decisions align with misery, create some that align with joy and happiness."

"Nurture your gifts and your gifts will nurture your success."

"Get naked, reveal and rebuild yourself."

"Make a decision, good or bad; all decisions are good decisions, you made them."

"Stop beating yourself up for not aligning with societal conditioning, and nurture yourself for stepping out the box."

"Stress is relieved by acknowledging the present moment."

"Always stand up when standing is not easy."

"You don't have to look like or act like you are experiencing hard times."

"Don't be afraid to show and wear your flaws as they are bigger than your mindset can see. Your shame and embarrassment hinders your inner and spiritual growth."

"Listen with the intent to learn and understand, not reply."

Business Quotes

"If we jumped as quickly to opportunities as we did conclusions, we would all be successful and wealthy."

"My success is only determined by my choices, not anyone else's."

"Confidence is the main ingredient for success."

"Be mindful of those who are only interested in you if they benefit from you."

"When selecting your team, be sure those people are aligned with your dream."

"Your business is your business, but to be successful, you must be nosy."

"Your attitude can make or break you, and if you believe that to be untrue, you just broke yourself."

"Sacrifice your settled thoughts for the sake of elevating you and your business."

"Great leaders put the interest of others at the center of their attention as it is not about them."

"Stepping on others to grow in business will only result in becoming a stepstool for someone else."

"The better your thoughts, the more successful your business."

"When you learn to accept constructive criticism you can then construct a better business."

"Every business started with a team, and every successful business requires a team to stay in business."

"The smartest businessman is the servant of the Universe who gets paid for doing what he loves."

"Delegation is required to improve your leadership skills."

"A business isn't something you work for, it is something you build."

"Your dreams will suffocate if you choose not to birth them."

"The cemetery is the richest place in the world and not because of the headstones, but because of the untold books, businesses, inventions, and otherwise."

Kelley Porter

"Reading the fine print is what educates you, ignoring it is what humiliates you."

"The desire to be successful and rich is personal, but the desire to change lives is spiritual."

"Appreciate the dollar you earn not what you spend it on."

"When you make a smart defensive move, there's no way your defensive team can lose."

Kelley Porter

Health Quotes

"The gap between disease and death is your mouth."

"Healing is a choice, dis-ease is optional."

"We can live without meat, but the worms in your body cannot."

"Failure to clean your colon will result in an obese and a diseased body."

"GMO's aren't killing us no more than guns are, we are when we choose to eat them and pull the trigger."

"Alkaline food to your body is like water to a flower."

"Dead meat is dead energy in a live body that will eventually become a dead body."

"Your colon is no different than a sewage system or toilet stool; it needs flushing."

"Eat with the intention to nurture and heal your body."

"Your health is your true source of wealth, not your job, business, cars, things or bling."

"We don't know the value of health until our bodies become diseased."

"You are not required to sacrifice your emotional or physical needs to satisfy someone else."

"The best workout you can ever complete is the one that results in sweating."

Kelley Porter

Abuse Quotes

"The average human tongue weighs between two and three ounces, but the impact of it can be life or death; speak life.

"When you harbor negative thoughts, you emotionally and physically abuse yourself."

"If you didn't like it when your parents called you stupid or dumb, why would behave like your parents?"

"President #45 is mentally, verbally and emotionally abusive to the people around the world, but he is also suffering deeply."

"I came from a very abusive and painful background, but I also came from a history of strength and greatness."

"If you can become angry when President #45 speaks ill about black people, you should be enraged after watching two teenagers abuse and brutally beat each other."

"Shame and embarrassment belong to the child molester."

"People call men or women that inflict pain an abusive person, but how do we describe the person who allowed it?"

Forgiveness Quotes

"When you choose not to forgive, you choose to remain a victim."

"Forgiveness is the greatest emotional success in the world."

"Forgiveness is a gift to you as you release the pain, bitterness, and resentment."

"Forgiveness frees your soul from the depths of darkness."

"Forgiveness cannot be accomplished if we never accept what happened."

"Forgiveness requires you to have compassion for those who projected pain onto you."

"The primary reason for your unhappiness is unforgiveness and ill thoughts about life's experiences."

"Forgiveness can heal a broken mindset."

"If you cannot have compassion for, and forgive self, it will be impossible to forgive others as everything begins with you."

"Forgiveness washes away all old things and brings about new things."

Featured Bonus
10 Ways to Release Negative Thoughts

10 Ways to Release Negative Thoughts

1. Acknowledge the thought:
It is impossible to release a negative thought if you refuse to acknowledge its existence. The purpose of recognizing the thought is to become aware of what you think. More importantly, there is no negative behavior without first negative thought. Acknowledge your thought by merely saying "I hear you" and then replace it with a positive thought.

2. Replace the negative thought with a positive thought:
When you think you are "fat" or "you will never be happy," counteract that thought by saying "I am thin and healthy" and I am always happy. Do not entertain the thought by creating an emotion as it will become your belief or life. Thoughts become things, as they follow an emotion that generates more energy surrounding the thought and bringing it to fruition.

3. Ask yourself: What am I thinking and what am I feeling:
The goal behind this is to bring your mind back to the present moment. When we are in deep thought it is because we are focused on the past or future and neither one of them are more important than the present moment. So ask yourself, "What am I thinking?" This will empower you to become conscious and redirect your thoughts to something more positive. Then ask yourself, "What am I feeling?" This will empower you to become conscious of any unhealthy emotions you may have created from the negative thought.

4. Don't internalize other people's words:
The last thing you should do is internalize what someone else thinks of you and make it yours. In the past, there were probably people who spoke harmful to you, and you believed them. Well, that is internalizing their thought or opinion of you. What others think of you is their business, not yours.

5. Speak affirmations into your life:
If you want to release negative thoughts, speak positive affirmations in your life. Use the two most powerful words, I AM and be sure something powerful and positive follows it. What follows I am, follows you.

I am beautiful
I am wealth

I am a health
I am supported by the Universe
I love and approve of myself
I believe in myself and my abilities
I always make the right choices
I learn from my mistakes and trust myself

Try the affirmations above, daily and add some that resonated with you. Positive only.

6. **Don't take the thought seriously:**
Too many of us allow our minds to wander off and without any supportive facts, we take the thoughts seriously. Have you ever witnessed someone go from smiling to frowning? Imagine what he or she is thinking about and how that person's thoughts have changed their entire mood. Thoughts are just that, and you can analyze yours and decide if you want to take the thought seriously or counteract with a positive thought.

7. **Don't blame others for your negative thinking:**
Placing blame denies you the opportunity to learn from pain and experiences. When you have negative thoughts, it is because you choose to think negative. More than half of our daily thoughts are negative, and you can consciously decide to think positive. But, please do not blame others for your negative thought process. Maybe you were raised in a negative environment and just carried that energy to your adult life, but no-one is responsible for you creating negative thoughts. Be accountable for your negative mindset and that way you have the desire to change it.

8. **Smile**:
Smiling is contagious as when you smile, it's clear that smile is accompanied by positive thoughts unless you're sarcastic or facetious. When you smile, there is a positive response that goes back to the brain and supports our feeling of joy. Smiling is like eating chocolate and inducing pleasure. Smile more as it stimulates positive thoughts and satisfaction.

9. **Surround yourself with positive people:**
We've heard this time and time again, and most people do not follow this simple rule. Negative minded people rub off on you. Transfer of energy is real, and negative people tend to rub off on others. If you continue to spend

time in their space, eventually you will begin to think and speak just like them. The first law of thermodynamics states that energy can neither be destroyed, nor created, but it can be transformed. Surround yourself with positive thinking people as those are the ones you want to rub off on you.

10. **List 10 things you are grateful for right now:**
- I'm alive
- I have good health
- I have wealth
- I help others heal
- I understand forgiveness
- I have compassion for others
- I have access to abundance
- I have a beautiful son
- I have a wonderful husband
- I have food, clothes, and shelter

ABOUT THE AUTHOR

A successful leader and expert on overcoming all forms of abuse, avoiding toxic relationships and the art of forgiveness, Kelley Porter is a Certified Transformation, and Personal Development Coach, Award Winning Five-time Author, and Professional Speaker. After completing a motivational speech in 2008, and witnessing the effect of her story, Perfectly Planned was born, a book about overcoming child molestation is not only inspirational and empowering; it is an amazing memoir that provides hope for the abused, knowledge for the unaware, and strength for survivors. Prior to Kelley's life purpose, she spent twenty-three years in healthcare and worked fifteen of those years as a Medical Technologist, and is a member of the American Society of Clinical Pathologist.

As a speaker, Kelley's transparent and authentic style of speaking will empower anyone to self-reflect, start the process of healing and correct thoughts and behaviors that may hinder them from living a healthy and non-toxic lifestyle.

As a Coach, Kelley empowers you to reach emotional freedom, gain clarity and discover your infinite possibilities. She is well known for assisting in the removal of mental and emotional blocks that hinders people from reaching their fullest potential. Her areas of specialty are, but not limited to; abuse, healing, relationships, thoughts, emotions, and behaviors as she has written books on all topics. Kelley has over thirty years of direct experience with all forms of abuse, domestic violence relationships, creating purpose and power from painful experiences, and creating a positive mindset.

Kelley contributes to society her genuine love for healing, improving awareness and identity, developing talents and potential; enhancing the quality of life and the realization of dreams and aspirations. Kelley's mission is to guide you to design a healthy and meaningful life through wisdom, consciousness, self-reflection, self-love, accountability and forgiveness.

Kelley has been seen and heard on radio and TV including WVON, HOT105 (Florida), Inspiration 1390, WKKC, Channel 2, 5, 7, 9 and 19 and My Black is Beautiful (online). She has been featured in Rolling Out Magazine, Chicago Tribune, Bean Soup Times, SisterSpeak237 (Africa) and spoken for numerous prestigious organizations such as Robert H. McKinney Law School and the Chicago Police Department. She is available for speaking engagements such as keynotes, seminars, workshops, conferences and panels. Her audience can range from congregations, universities, youth groups, NFP and community organizations, the educational and prison system as well as shelters.

Kelley Porter

www.ingramcontent.com/pod-product-compliance
Lightning Source LLC
Chambersburg PA
CBHW020110020526

44112CB00033B/1140